Favorite
HYMNS
and High Contrast Photographs

D1209197

HARVARD RANCH PUBLISHING
Harvard Ranch Series - Book 3

Harvard Ranch Publishing
P.O. Box 842
Kalispell, MT 59903

Printed in the United States of America

Library of Congress Cataloging-in-Publication Data
Reinhold, Kathy editor
          Favorite Hymns
    Large print hymns / edited by Kathy Reinhold, Laura Donavan,
William S. Donavan— 1st ed.
1. Large Print 2. Hymns 3. Elderly
Very large print (48 pt) hard cover book with high contrast
photographs and familiar hymns for those with low vision.

Library of Congress Cataloging-in-Publication Number 99-60165
ISBN 1-893630-27-7

Acknowledgments

This book would not have been possible without the help of many people. We would especially like to thank

Pickles McKinley, Buena Vista, CO
Pastor Fred Dare, Buena Vista, CO
Dr. Thomas W. Theune, Colorado Springs, CO
Frances Leif Neer, San Francisco, CA
The Lighthouse, San Francisco, CA
The Lighthouse, New York, NY
Dot Kellar, Creative Care Center, Cocoa Beach, FL
Melanie Goff, Autumn House, Melbourne, FL
Charlotte Millspaugh, Brevard Alzheimer's Foundation, Melbourne, FL
Dian Williamson, Corwin Center, Redmond, WA
Susanne Buckalew, Leslie Donavan, Sue Frank, Christine Funcik,
Ben Long, Laura Munson, Karen Nichols, Marcia Phillips,
Lyman Rowan and Dave Stone for their editing, writing, and proofreading
Roland and Jane Cheek for their publishing expertise
Trudy, Photo Video Plus, and "rock star Ken" at Inland
Mom for being patient, and all our awesome friends in the Flathead
Dad for teaching me that creating books and distributing books are different projects
Digital Planet for amazing scans as well as their help with color manipulation
Penny Williams for her sensitive insights
Florence Jones, our inspiration

Florence and Elena sharing a book

A Mighty Fortress Is Our God

A mighty fortress
is our God,
A bulwark never failing;
Our helper He
amid the flood
Of mortal ills prevailing.

Martin Luther

1

All Things Bright and Beautiful

All things
bright and beautiful,
All creatures
great and small,
All things
wise and wonderful,
The Lord God
made them all.

Cecil F. Alexander

3

Amazing Grace

Amazing grace!
how sweet the sound,
That saved a wretch
like me!
I once was lost, but
now am found,
Was blind, but
now I see.

John Newton

Bringing in the Sheaves

Sowing in the morning,
sowing seeds of kindness,
Sowing in the noontide
and the dewy eve;
Waiting for the harvest,
and the time of reaping,
We shall come rejoicing,
bringing in the sheaves.

Knowles Shaw

Fairest Lord Jesus

Fairest Lord Jesus,
Ruler of all nature,
O Thou of God
and man the Son,
Thee will I cherish,
Thee will I honor,
Thou my soul's glory,
joy, and crown.

Author Unknown

9

Father, We Thank Thee for the Night

Father, we thank Thee
for the night,
And for the pleasant
morning light,
For rest and food
and loving care,
And all that makes
the day so fair.

Rebecca J. Weston

For the Beauty of the Earth

For the beauty of the earth,
For the glory of the skies,
For the love which
from our birth
Over and around us lies:
Christ our God,
to Thee we raise
This our hymn
of grateful praise.

Folliott S. Pierpoint

God Be With You

God be with you
till we meet again,
By His counsels guide,
uphold you,
With His sheep
securely fold you;
God be with you
till we meet again.

J. E. Rankin

Holy, Holy, Holy! Lord God Almighty

Holy, holy, holy!
Lord God Almighty!
Early in the morning
our song shall rise
to Thee;
Holy, holy, holy!
merciful and mighty;
God in three persons,
blessed Trinity!

Reginald Heber

17

How Great Thou Art

O Lord my God!
When I in
awesome wonder
Consider all the worlds
Thy hands have made,
I see the stars,
I hear the rolling thunder,
Thy pow'r throughout the
universe displayed...

Stuart K. Hine

19

I Love to Tell the Story

I love to tell the story
Of unseen things above,
Of Jesus and his glory,
Of Jesus and his love.
I love to tell the story,
Because I know it's true;
It satisfies my longings
As nothing else would do.

Katherine Hankey

In the Garden

I come to the garden alone,
While the dew
is still on the roses;
And the voice I hear,
Falling on my ear;
The Son of God discloses.
And He walks with me,
and He talks with me,
And He tells me I am
His own...

C. Austin Miles

Just a Closer Walk with Thee

Just a closer walk
with Thee,
Grant it, Jesus, is my plea,
Daily walking
close to Thee,
Let it be, dear Lord,
let it be.

Author Unknown

25

Morning Has Broken

Morning has broken
Like the first morning,
Blackbird has spoken
Like the first bird.
Praise for the singing!
Praise for the morning!
Praise for them, springing
Fresh from the Word!

Eleanor Farjeon

O God, Our Help in Ages Past

O God, our help
in ages past,
Our hope for years
to come,
Our shelter from the
stormy blast,
And our eternal home!

Isaac Watts

The Old Rugged Cross

So I'll cherish
the old rugged cross,...
Till my trophies
at last I lay down;
I will cling to
the old rugged cross,...
And exchange it some
day for a crown.

George Bennard

Peace Like a River

I've got peace like a river,
I've got peace like a river,
I've got peace like a river
in my soul.
I've got love like an ocean,
I've got love like an ocean,
I've got love like an ocean
in my soul.

Author Unknown

Praise God From Whom All Blessings Flow

Praise God from whom
all blessings flow;
Praise him, all creatures
here below;
Praise him above, ye
heavenly host:
Praise Father, Son, and
Holy Ghost. Amen.

Thomas Ken

Sabbath Prayer

May the Lord protect and
defend you.
May He always shield you
from shame.
May you come to be
in Israel a shining name.

Author Unknown

Shall We Gather at the River?

Shall we gather
at the river,
Where bright angel feet
have trod;
With its crystal
tide forever
Flowing by the throne
of God?

Rev. Robert Lowry

Sweet By and By

In the sweet by and by,
We shall meet on that
beautiful shore;
In the sweet by and by,
We shall meet on that
beautiful shore.

S.F. Bennett

41

This Is My Father's World

This is my Father's world;
And to my listening ears,
All nature sings,
and round me rings
The music of the spheres.
This is my Father's world;
I rest me in the thought
Of rocks and trees,
of skies and seas,
His hand the wonders
wrought.

Maltbie D. Babcock

43

We Gather Together

We gather together to
ask the Lord's blessing,
He chastens and hastens
His will to make known;
The wicked oppressing
cease them from
distressing,
Sing praises to His name,
He forgets not His own.

Author Unknown

45

What a Friend

What a friend we have
in Jesus,
All our sins and griefs
to bear!
What a privilege to carry
Everything to God
in prayer!

Joseph Scriven

Additional Hymn Verses

1 A Mighty Fortress is Our God

A mighty fortress is our God,
A bulwark never failing;
Our helper He amid the flood
Of mortal ills prevailing.
For still our ancient foe
Doth seek to work us woe—
His craft and pow'r are great,
And, armed with cruel hate,
On earth is not his equal.
*photo Bill Donavan - Cape Blanco
Lighthouse, Oregon*

3 All Things Bright and Beautiful

All things bright and beautiful,
All creatures great and small,
All things wise and wonderful,
The Lord God made them all.
Each little flower that opens,
Each little bird that sings,
He made their glowing colors,
He made their tiny wings.
*photo Karen Nichols - Mountain Goat,
Montana*

5 Amazing Grace

Amazing Grace!
How sweet the sound,
That saved a wretch like me!
I once was lost, but now am found,
Was blind, but now I see.

'Twas grace that taught my heart to fear,
And grace my fears relieved;
How precious did that grace appear
The hour I first believed!
*photo Bill Donavan - cowboy Paul,
Harvard Ranch, Colorado*

7 Bringing In the Sheaves

Sowing in the morning,
Sowing seeds of kindness,
Sowing in the noontide and
the dewy eve;
Waiting for the harvest,
and the time of reaping,
We shall come rejoicing,
bringing in the sheaves.
Bringing in the sheaves,
bringing in the sheaves,
We shall come rejoicing,
bringing in the sheaves.
photo Bill Donavan - Montana wheat

9 Fairest Lord Jesus

Fairest Lord Jesus, Ruler of all nature,
O Thou of God and man the Son,
Thee will I cherish, Thee will I honor,
Thou my soul's glory, joy, and crown.

Fair are the meadows,
Fairer still the woodlands,
Robed in the blooming garb of spring;
Jesus is fairer, Jesus is purer,
Who makes the woeful heart to sing.
*photo Tracy Stark - North Carolina
Chapel*

11 Father, We Thank Thee for the Night

Father, we thank thee for the night,
And for the pleasant morning light,
For rest and food and loving care,
And all that makes the day so fair.

Help us to do the things we should,
To be to others kind and good,

In all we do in work or play,
To grow more loving every day.
photo Bill Donavan - Laura and Shea sunning, Rockledge, Florida

13 For the Beauty of the Earth

For the beauty of the earth,
For the glory of the skies,
For the love which from our birth
Over and around us lies:
Christ our God, to Thee we raise
This our hymn of grateful praise.

For the wonder of each hour
Of the day and of the night,
Hill and vale and tree and flower,
Sun and moon and stars of light:
Christ our God, to Thee we raise
This our hymn of grateful praise.
photo Rita Fitzsimmons - Annecy, France

15 God Be with You

God be with you till we meet again,
By His counsels guide, uphold you,
With His sheep securely fold you;
God be with you till we meet again.

God be with you till we meet again,
'Neath His wings protecting
hide you,
Daily manna still provide you;
God be with you till we meet again.
photo Ross Cruden - Mark and Ruby, Rockledge, Florida

17 Holy, holy, holy! Lord God Almighty

Holy, holy, holy! Lord God Almighty!
Early in the morning
our song shall rise to Thee;
Holy, holy, holy! Merciful and mighty;
God in three persons, Blessed Trinity!

Holy, holy, holy! all the saints
adore Thee,
Casting down their golden crowns
around the glassy sea;
Cherubim and Seraphim,
falling down before Thee,
Which wert, and art, and evermore
shalt be.
photo - Gary Boorom, St. Mark's Choir, Cocoa, Florida

19 How Great Thou Art

O Lord my God!
When I in awesome wonder
Consider all the worlds
Thy hands have made;
I see the stars,
I hear the rolling thunder,
Thy pow'r throughout the
universe displayed;

Then sings my soul,
my Savior God to Thee;
How great Thou art, how great
Thou art!
Then sings my soul,
my Savior God to Thee;
How great Thou art,
how great Thou art.
photo Kevin O'Connell - Sunflower

21 I Love to Tell the Story

I love to tell the story
Of unseen things above,
Of Jesus and his glory,
Of Jesus and his love.
I love to tell the story,
Because I know it's true;
It satisfies my longings
As nothing else would do.

I love to tell the story;
'Twill be my theme in glory
To tell the old, old story
Of Jesus and his love.

I love to tell the story,
For those who know it best
Seem hungering and thirsting
To hear it, like the rest.

And when, in scenes of glory,
I sing the new, new song,
'Twill be the old, old story
That I have loved so long.
photo Bill Donavan - Poppie and Phoebe reading, Whitefish, Montana

23 In the Garden

I come to the garden alone,
While the dew is still on the roses;
And the voice I hear,
Falling on my ear;
The Son of God discloses.

And He walks with me,
and He talks with me,
And He tells me I am His own;
And the joy we share as we tarry there,
None other has ever known.

He speaks, and the sound of His voice
Is so sweet the birds hush their
singing, And the melody
That He gave to me
Within my heart is ringing.
photo Bill Donavan - rose, Montana

25 Just a Closer Walk with Thee

I am weak, but Thou art strong,
Jesus, keep me from all wrong;
I'll be satisfied as long (just as long)
As I walk, let me walk close to Thee.

Just a closer walk with Thee,
Grant it, Jesus, is my plea,
Daily walking close to Thee,
Let it be, dear Lord, let it be.
photo Tracy Stark - Terry and Sydney on the North Carolina coast

27 Morning Has Broken

Morning has broken
Like the first morning,
Blackbird has spoken
Like the first bird.
Praise for the singing!
Praise for the morning!
Praise for them, springing
Fresh from the Word!

Sweet the rain's new fall
Sunlit from heaven,
Like the first dew fall
On the first grass.
Praise for the sweetness
Of the wet garden,
Sprung in completeness
Where his feet pass.
photo Karen Nichols - Yellow headed blackbird, Ninepipe Reservoir, Montana

29 O God, Our Help in Ages Past

O God, our help in ages past,
Our hope for years to come,
Our shelter from the stormy blast,
And our eternal home!

Under the shadow of Thy throne
Thy saints have dwelt secure;
Sufficient is Thine arm alone,
And our defense is sure.
photo Bill Donavan - St. Matthew's Church, Kalispell, Montana

31 The Old Rugged Cross

On a hill far away stood an
old rugged cross,
The emblem of suffering and shame;
And I love that old cross
where the dearest and best
For a world of lost sinners was slain.

So I'll cherish the old rugged cross,...
Till my trophies at last I lay down.
I will cling to the old rugged cross,...
And exchange it some day for a
crown.
photo Ross Cruden -banana leaf, Rockledge, Florida

33 Peace Like a River

I've got peace like a river,
I've got peace like a river,
I've got peace like a river in my soul.
I've got love like an ocean,
I've got love like an ocean,
I've got love like an ocean in my soul.
I've got joy like a fountain,
I've got joy like a fountain,
I've got joy like a fountain in my soul.
photo Bill Donavan - Pacific Ocean, Southern Oregon

35 Praise God From Whom All Blessings Flow

Praise God from whom
all blessings flow;
Praise him, all creatures here below;
Praise him above, ye heavenly host:
Praise Father, Son, and Holy Ghost.
Amen.
photo Ross Cruden - St. Francis garden statue, Rockledge, Florida

37 Sabbath Prayer

May the Lord protect and defend you.
May He always shield you from
shame.
May you come to be in
Israel a shining name.

May you be like Ruth and like Esther.
May you be deserving of praise.
Strengthen them, Oh Lord,
and keep them from the stranger's
ways.
photo Bill Donavan - Mike at Flathead Lake, Montana

39 Shall We Gather at the River?

Shall we gather at the river,
Where bright angel feet have trod;
With its crystal tide forever
Flowing by the throne of God?

Yes, we'll gather at the river,
The beautiful, the beautiful river;
Gather with the saints at the river
That flows by the throne of God.
photo Bill Donavan - McDonald Creek, Glacier National Park, Montana

41 Sweet By and By

There's a land that is fairer than day,
And by faith we can see it afar;
For the Father waits over the way,
To prepare us a dwelling place there.

In the sweet by and by,
We shall meet on that beautiful
shore;
In the sweet by and by,
We shall meet on that beautiful
shore.
*photo Kathy Nelson - Starfish,
San Diego, California*

43 This Is My Father's World

This is my Father's world;
And to my listening ears,
All nature sings,
and round me rings
The music of the spheres.
This is my Father's world;
I rest me in the thought
Of rocks and trees,
of skies and seas,
His hand the wonders wrought.
*photo Karen Nichols - Glacier
National Park, Montana*

45 We Gather Together

We gather together to
ask the Lord's blessing,
He chastens and hastens
His will to make known;
The wicked oppressing
cease them from distressing,
Sing praises to His name,
He forgets not His own.

Beside us to guide us,
our God with us joining
Ordaining, maintaining
His kingdom divine;
So from the beginning
the fight we were winning,
Thou, Lord, wast at our side,
the glory be Thine!
*photo Gary Boorom - Candace and
Kay, Rockledge, Florida*

47 What a Friend

What a Friend we have in Jesus,
All our sins and griefs to bear!
What a privilege to carry
Everything to God in prayer!

Have we trials and temptations?
Is there trouble anywhere?
We should never be discouraged,
Take it to the Lord in prayer.
*photo Bill Donavan - Karen
Nichols at St. Matthew's, Kalispell,
Montana*

The Harvard Ranch

Nothing stirs memories or lifts the spirit like the fondly remembered words and melodies of favorite songs. For many of us, no songs are more special than the hymns we learned as children and have sung throughout our lives.

Favorite Hymns is the third in a series of books published by Harvard Ranch Publishing. It is also one of our favorites.

The Harvard Ranch has been our family getaway for over 25 years. The rustic log home and outbuildings are nestled at the base of Mount Harvard in the Arkansas River Valley of central Colorado.

My sisters and I spent our summers exploring along Frenchmen's Creek and traipsing through the hills looking for wild berries and arrowheads. Today, the homestead is still just as wonderful as it was then, with its rushing creek, abundant wildlife, many dogs and fond memories. It has also been a great place to work on books.

My mother, inspired during an outing with a visually impaired friend, came up with the idea for this series of books. My parents, Kathy and Paul Reinhold, have often tackled difficult humanitarian and conservation projects. Designing and publishing a series of books was something entirely new for them. That is where my husband, Bill, and I stepped into the picture. As graphic designers, we were the next link in the chain connecting inspiration and creation. The result is this book.

Kathy and Laura

As is so common these days, our family is scattered across the country, but never do we feel more complete than in those grand and noisy times when we are all together at the ranch. There, life seems its most full.

In these pages, we hope to convey that same love of life. Thank you for selecting Harvard Ranch books. We hope you'll contact us with your comments or suggestions.

Laura